A Humblebees Christmas

Jingle All the Way

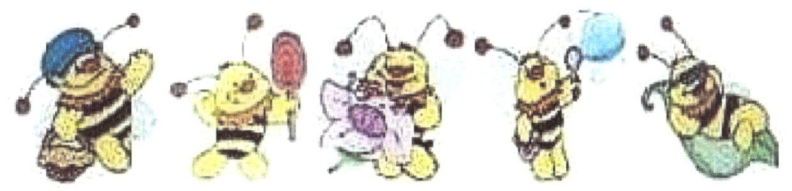

By

Cheryl Powe

Contents

Ch. 1 Winter Wonderland

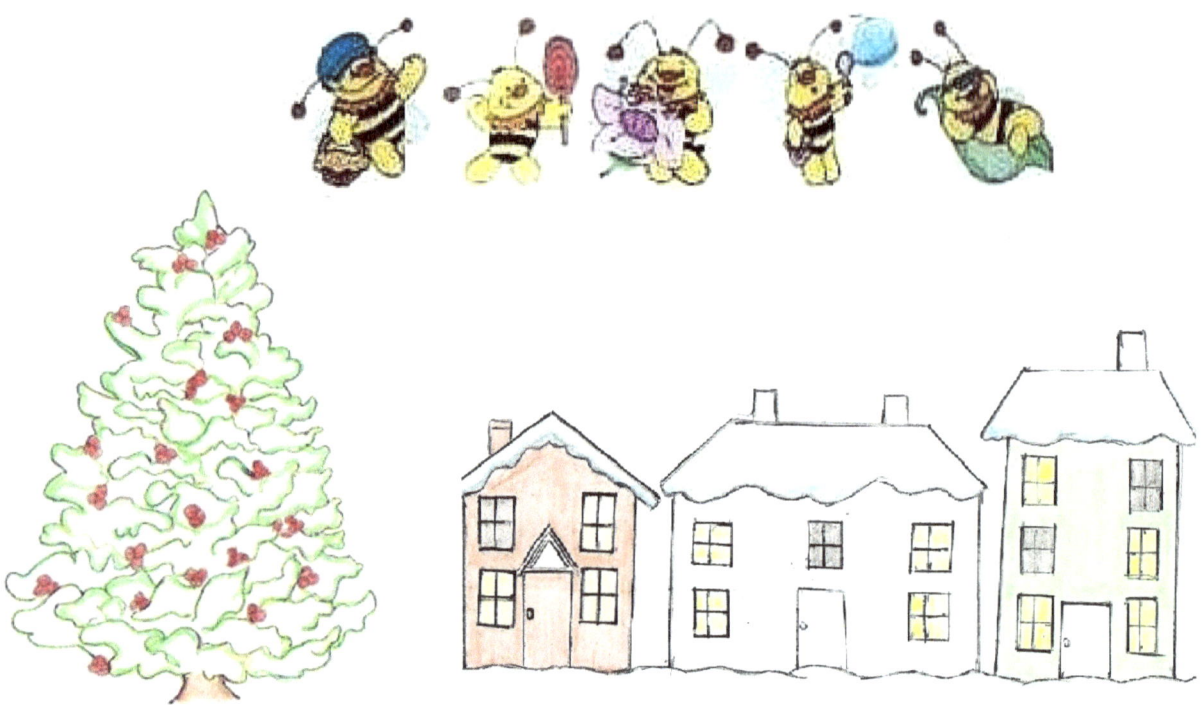

As the flakes began to fall fast from the sky, it covered the entire town with a blanket of snow. It gave this place a winter wonderland like it has never seen before. This is the time of year when coats, scarfs and mittens are needed to ward off the cold wind; this is the time of year called Christmas.

Underneath the branches of the snow covered trees laid a small but well protected bee hive. It was the home where the Humblebees stayed.

As Starry peeked out of the hive, he shyly flew back away from the opening and said "Hey everyone, it's snowing very hard outside and it's very cold, I think today might be a good day to stay indoors." Everyone nodded and agree that it looked like this was one of those cold winter days that happens every Christmas Eve.

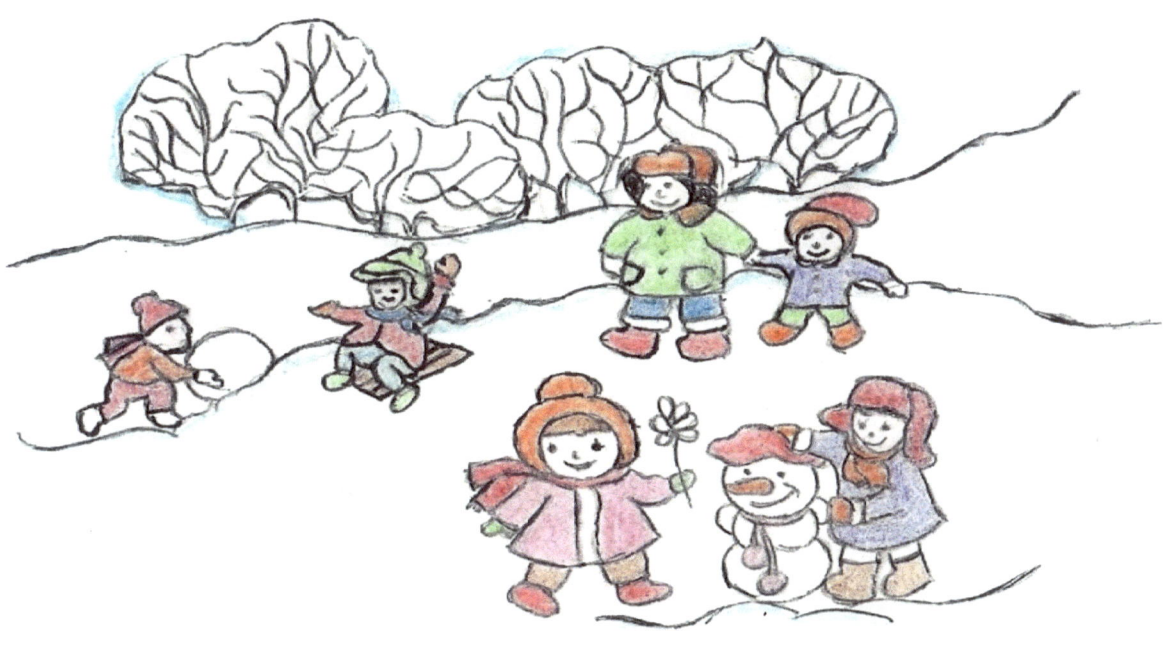

The Children

While the Humblebees were keeping warm inside of their hive, the sounds of children's laughter was heard from the park that was around the corner. They were building snowmen, sliding on sleds and catching snowflakes as they gingerly fell from the sky.

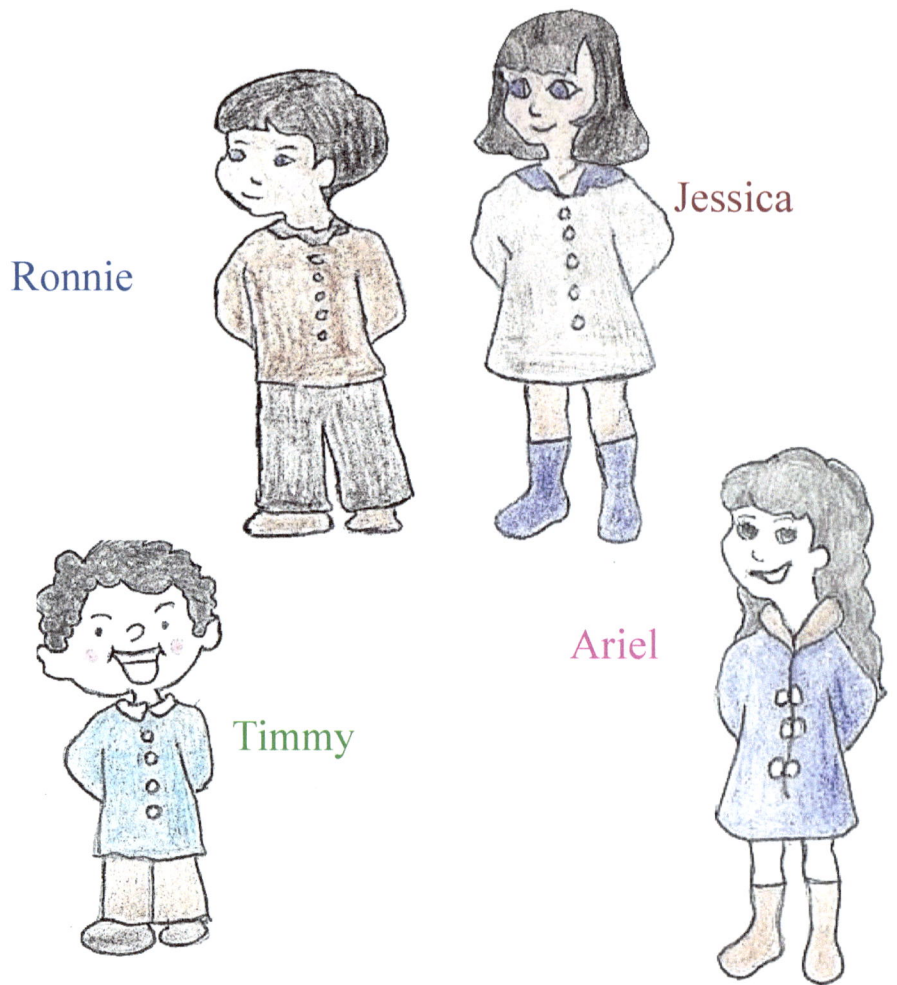

Ronnie

Jessica

Timmy

Ariel

Little Ronnie and his sister Jessica were enjoying themselves playing with the snow along with their friends, Ariel and Timmy. "I betcha I can build a bigger snowman than the rest of you, said Jessica. "Uh un, no you can't, I can build one bigger than anybody else in the whole wide world yelled Ariel.

Ronnie brought more snow and whispered "Here Jessica, use this to make it bigger, ok? "Alright, bring some more so that Ariel won't be able to catch up with me!" After more than an hour or so of playing Jessica and Ronnie had to say goodbye because they were going to visit their grandmother for Christmas.

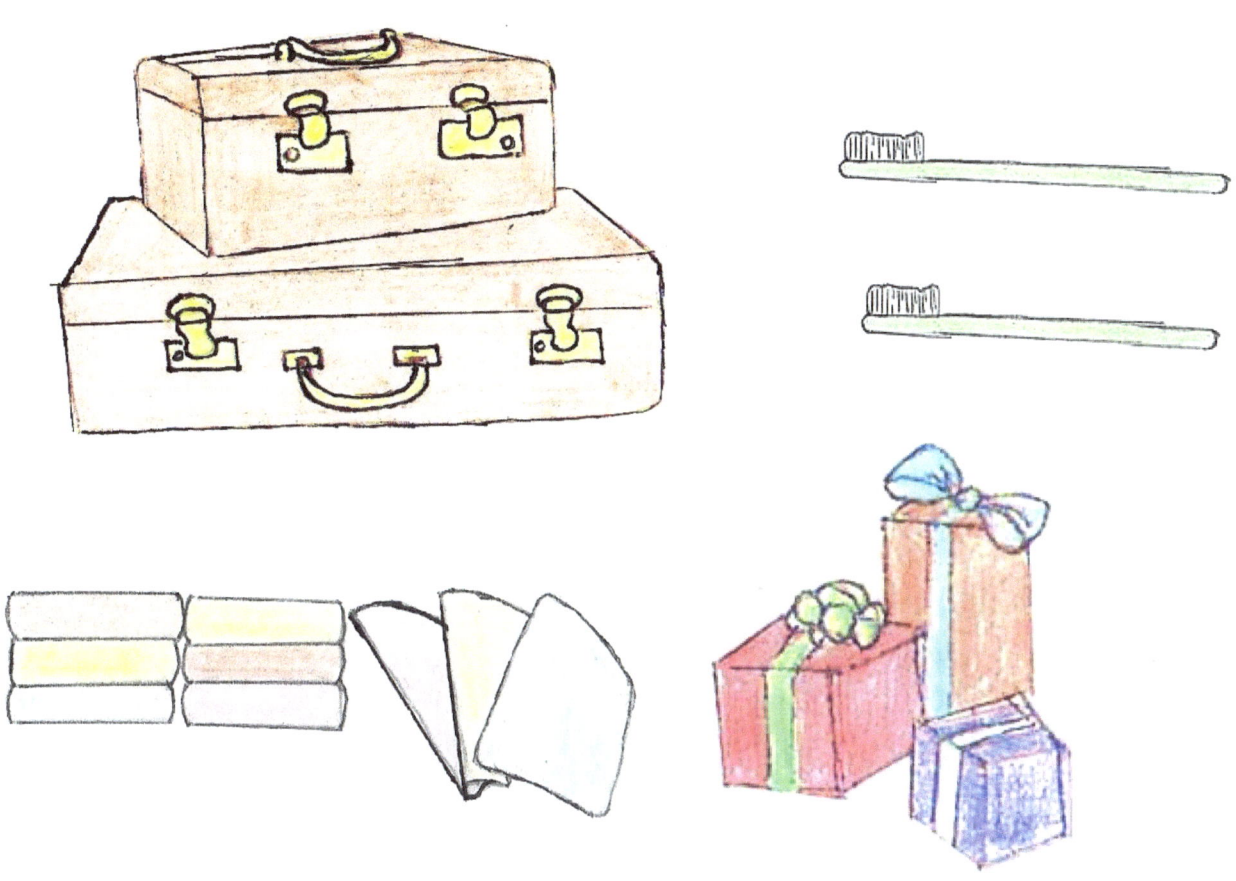

As Jessica and Ronnie arrived home, their parents were busy packing some clothes and Christmas presents for the trip to Grandma's house. After they went to their rooms, their mother Mrs. Hunter asked them to finish packing the rest of their clothes for the trip.

"Jessica, Ronnie; remember to pack your toothbrushes and towels ok? "Alright mom, we got 'em, we're almost done packing and ready to go" they both answered. C'mon everyone, it's time to go; let's leave now while the snow is slowing up a bit, said Mr. Hunter. Mrs. Hunter, Jessica and Ronnie brought their bags out and began to pile into the car.

Ch. 2 Let's have some fun too!

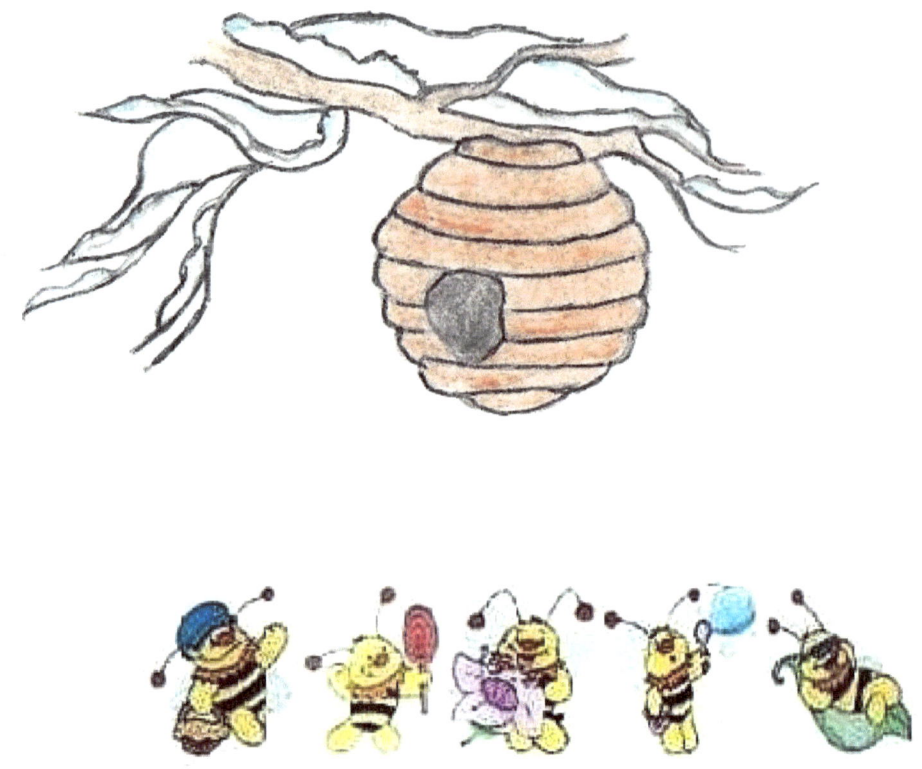

Since the snow had started to slow up a bit, it gave the Humblebees a chance to come outside and play. "I'm so glad that we could come out and play especially in all of this snow, sighed Beanie." "Yeah me too, let's have a lot of fun before it starts up again!" yelled Jimmy. The Humblebees flew out of the hive and into the wind and through the snow.

They were flying through the trees and bushes as their wings brushed up against the limbs while knocking the dust of snow down to the ground. "Oh wow, this is so much fun, let's do it again and again!! "Weeee, hurry up try and catch me if you can," Starry said.

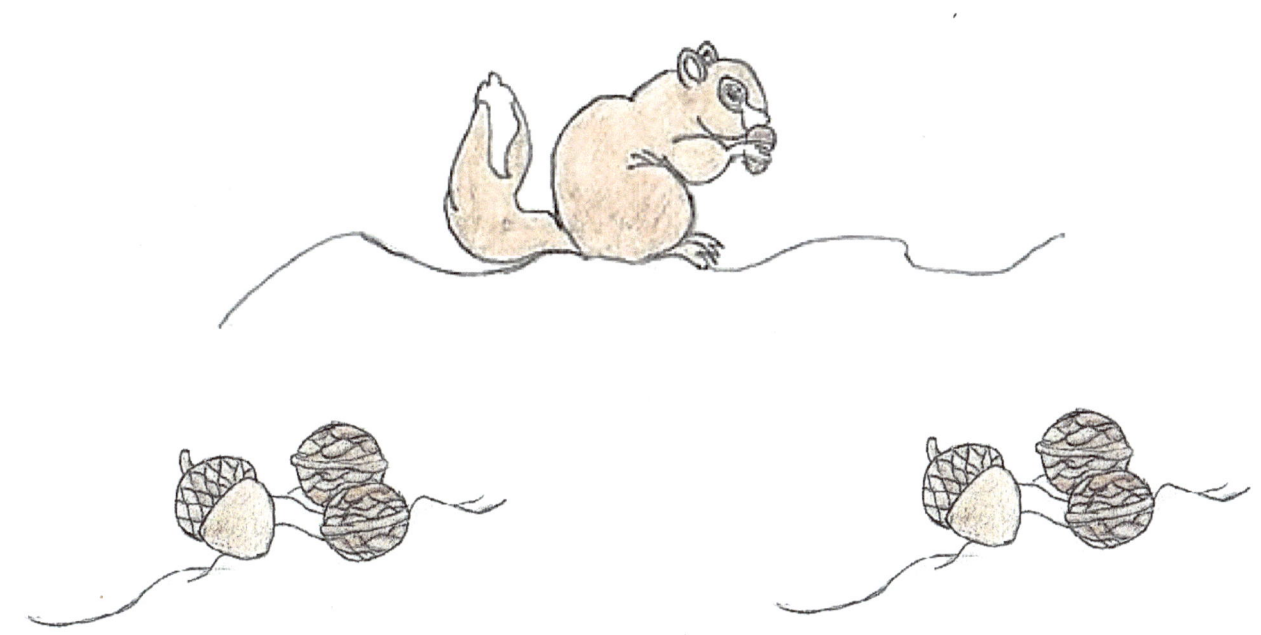

Jerry the squirrel gathering all of his nuts!

While playing, they ran into "Jerry" the squirrel who was busy gathering nuts from the trees. "Hey Jerry, you wanna play in the snow with us for a little while"? yelled Beanie. Sure Jerry answered, I'll play with you!" "Whoa, watch out below, coming in for a landing," yelled out Tiny who sounded like an airplane that was coming in to land.

Jerry and the rest of the squirrels joined in, ducking in and out of holes playing hide and seek with the Humblebees. Everyone was having so much fun that they lost track of time as the snow began to come down heavy once again.

"Uh oh, we better hurry back to the hive guys; it's starting to snow all over again, Jimmy said. Ok, see ya, Jerry! said Tiny. "See ya later! Humblebees.

Ch. 3 Over the River and through the woods!

"♫The horse knows the way, to carry the sleigh, through white and drifted snow, oh"! ♫

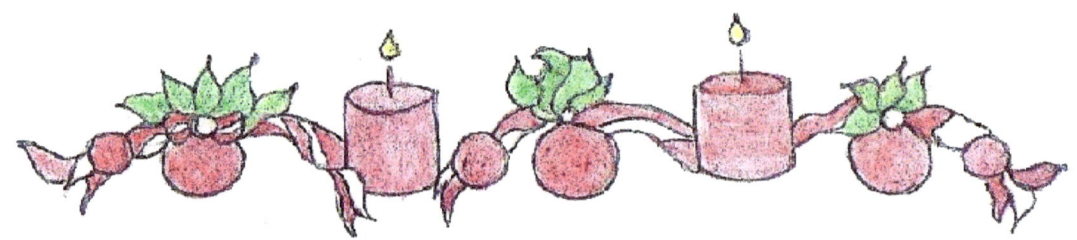

It was evening time as Jessica, Ronnie and their parents were well on their way to Grandma's house when the snow started to come down quickly again. As the car became covered, Mr. Hunter turned on his windshield wipers and headlights so that he could see better.

While riding, Mrs. Hunter came up with an idea to sing a song to help past the time from the long ride.

"♫Over the river and through the woods to grandmothers house we go, the horse knows the way, to carry the sleigh, through white and drifted snow, oh! Over the river and through the woods to have a full day of play. Oh, hear the bells ringing, ting-a-ling-ling, for it is Christmas Day, ♫.

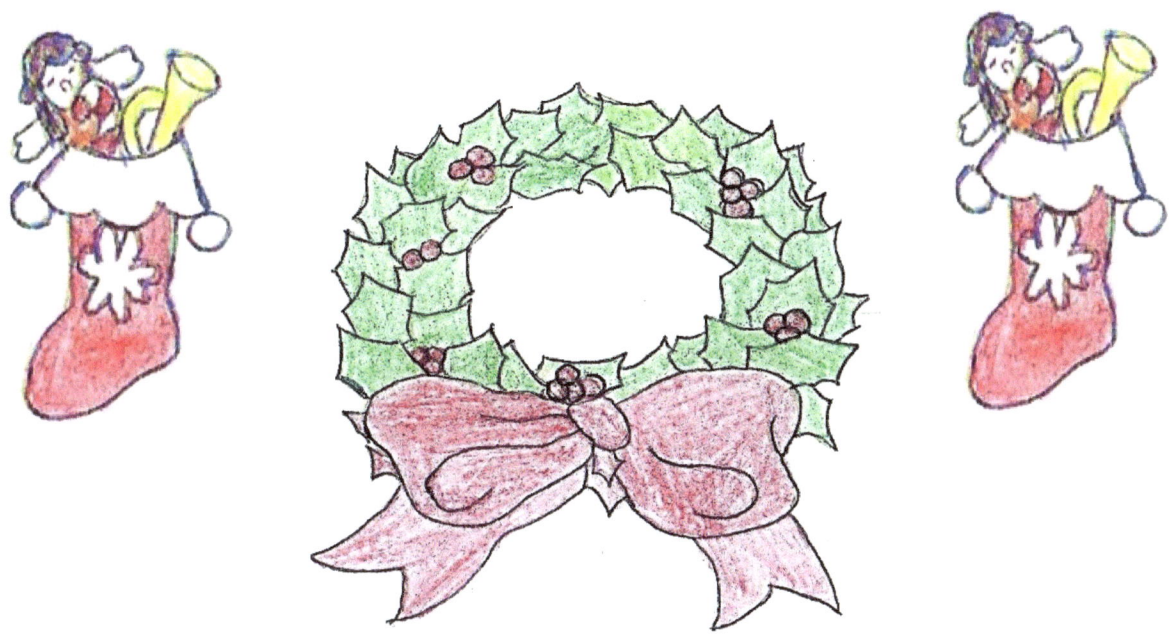

♫Dashing through the Snow, in a one horse open sleigh! ♫

Then there was another song that they decided to sing ♫*"Dashing through the snow, in a one horse open sleigh, o'er the hills we go, laughing all the way! Bells are bobtail ring, making spirits bright, oh what fun to laugh and sing a sleighing song tonight, oh Jingle Bells"♫*

As the snow continued to come down, Mr. Hunter notice that the car was driving slower. He thought that it was the snow on the road making the car act this way but it wasn't.

All of a sudden everyone stopped singing to watch the car. Soon he had to pull over to the side of the road and the car came to a complete stop.

Ch. 4 Stranded

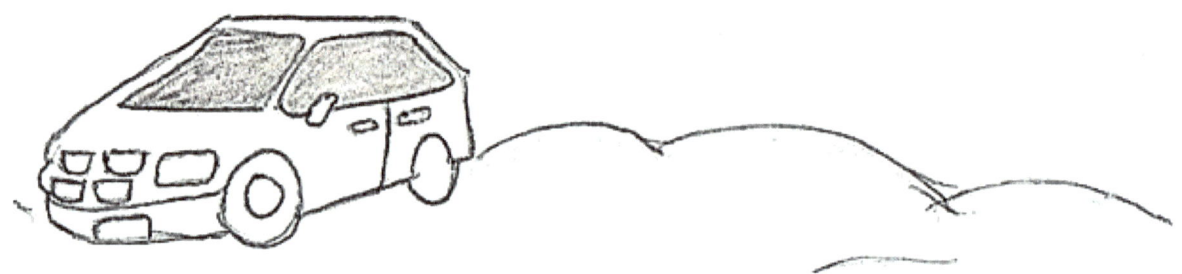

"Oh my goodness, what's wrong with the car?" asked Mrs. Hunter. "I think that I got a flat tire and I don't have a flashlight to change it" said Mr. Hunter. They waited and waited for someone to stop and help but the road had become empty. People were rushing to get home on Christmas Eve, one of the busiest times of the year.

Mr. and Mrs. Hunter, Jessica and Ronnie were getting closer to stay warm in the darkness and coldness of the night. "Aachoo!! was the sound of Ronnie sneezing; Mrs. Hunter spread out a blanket that she brought to help cover the children as the heater went out too. It was getting colder as time passed by and although the road was empty, they still had hopes of seeing someone who could help them on their way.

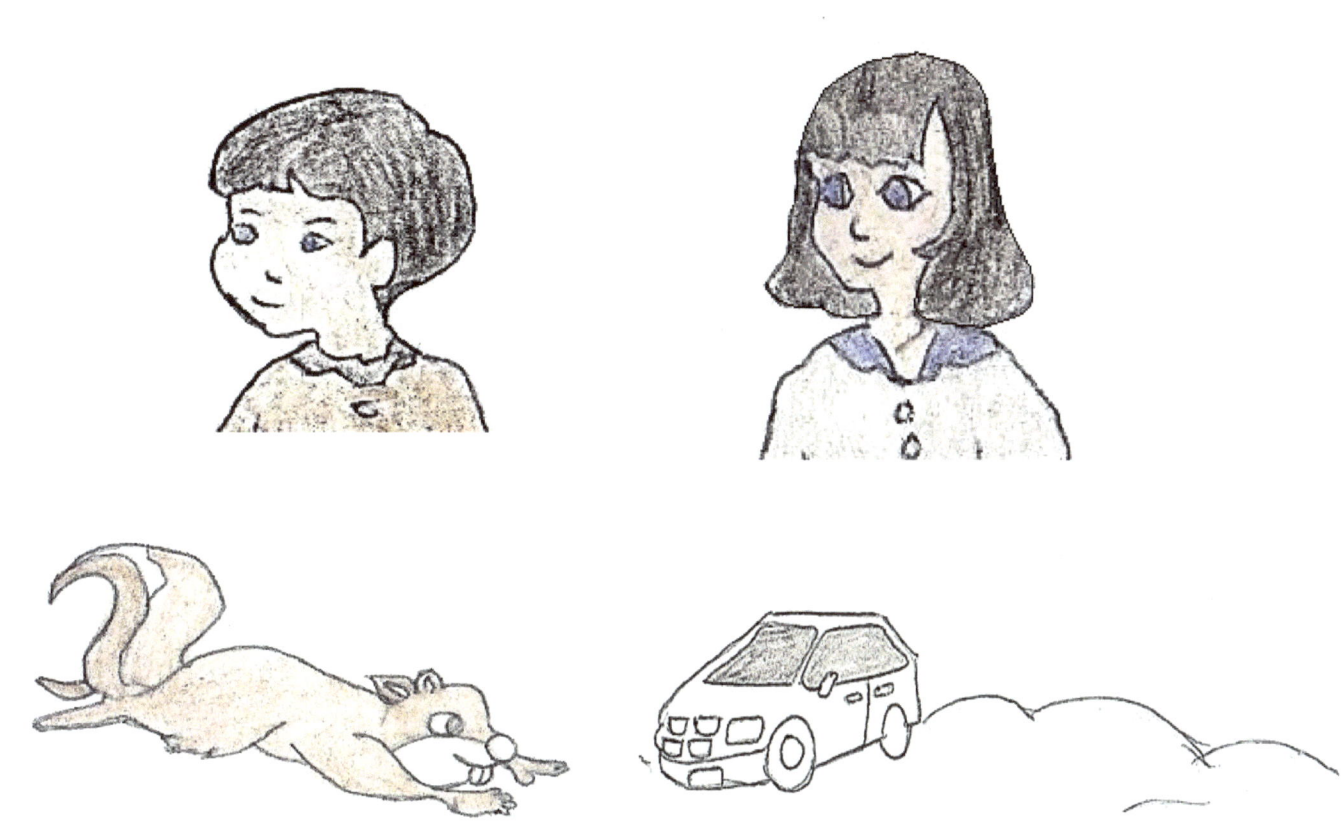

"I'm getting colder, how much longer will we have to wait before someone comes to help us"? Cried Ronnie. "Are we going to miss Christmas with grandma?" said Jessica. "We're not sure yet, I'm going to try and drive the car again said Mr. Hunter. While Mr. Hunter tried to
move the car, something tapped on the back window and got their attention.

"What was that noise? asked Jessica. "I don't know" said Ronnie. "Whatever it was, I think it ran away" he further explained. Unbeknownst to them, it was Jerry the squirrel who had tapped on the window to see if everything was ok. Jerry could sense danger whenever it was around and knew that he needed to get help from somewhere else.

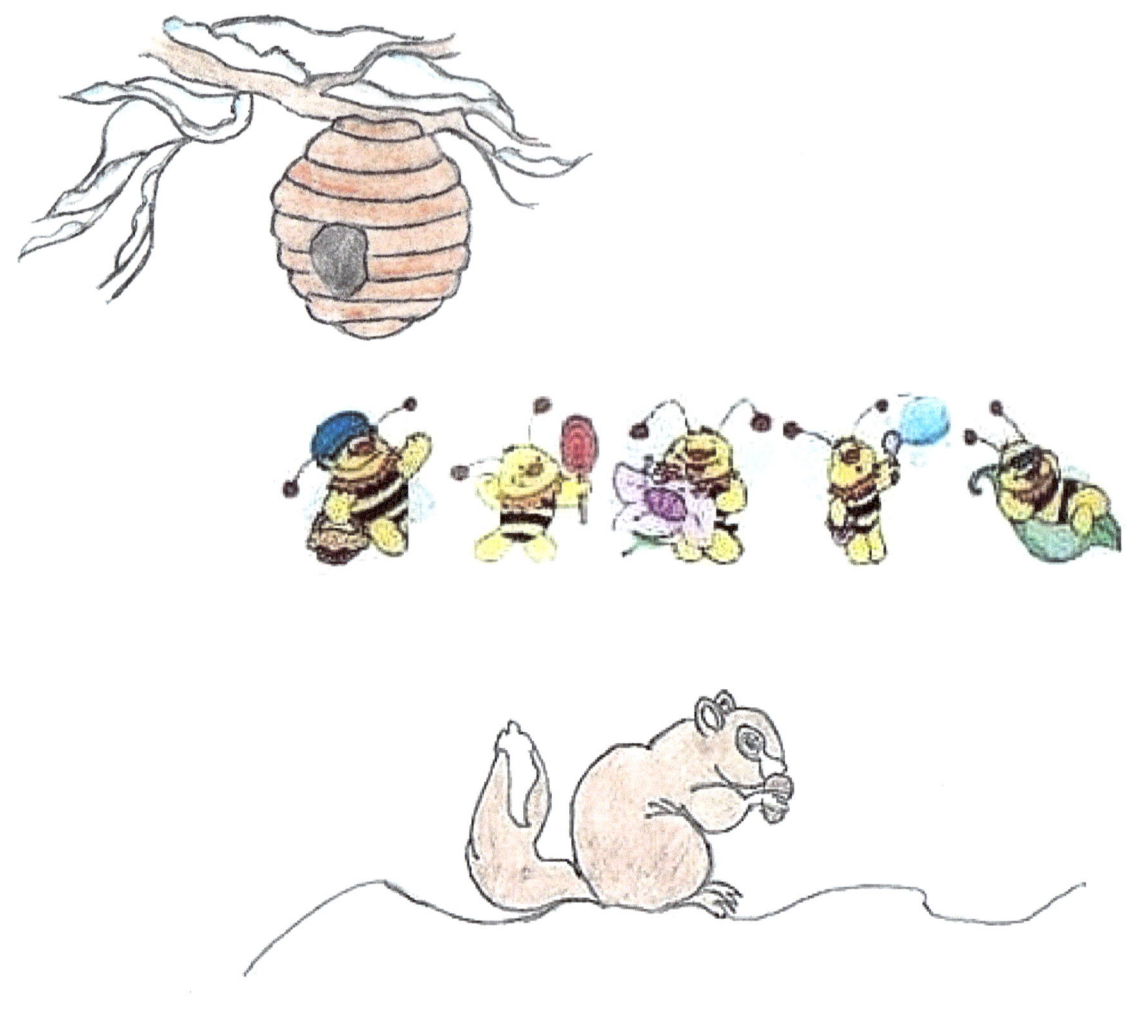

He remembered that he was playing with the Humblebees earlier and decided to run all the way back into town to tell them about what happened. He ran through the forest, the trees, bushes and the street.

He ran as fast as he could until he finally came back into town. Once he reached the Humblebees beehive he yelled out their names, Starry, Jimmy, Queeny, Beanie and Tiny!! Please come out; some people are in trouble and they need your help!!

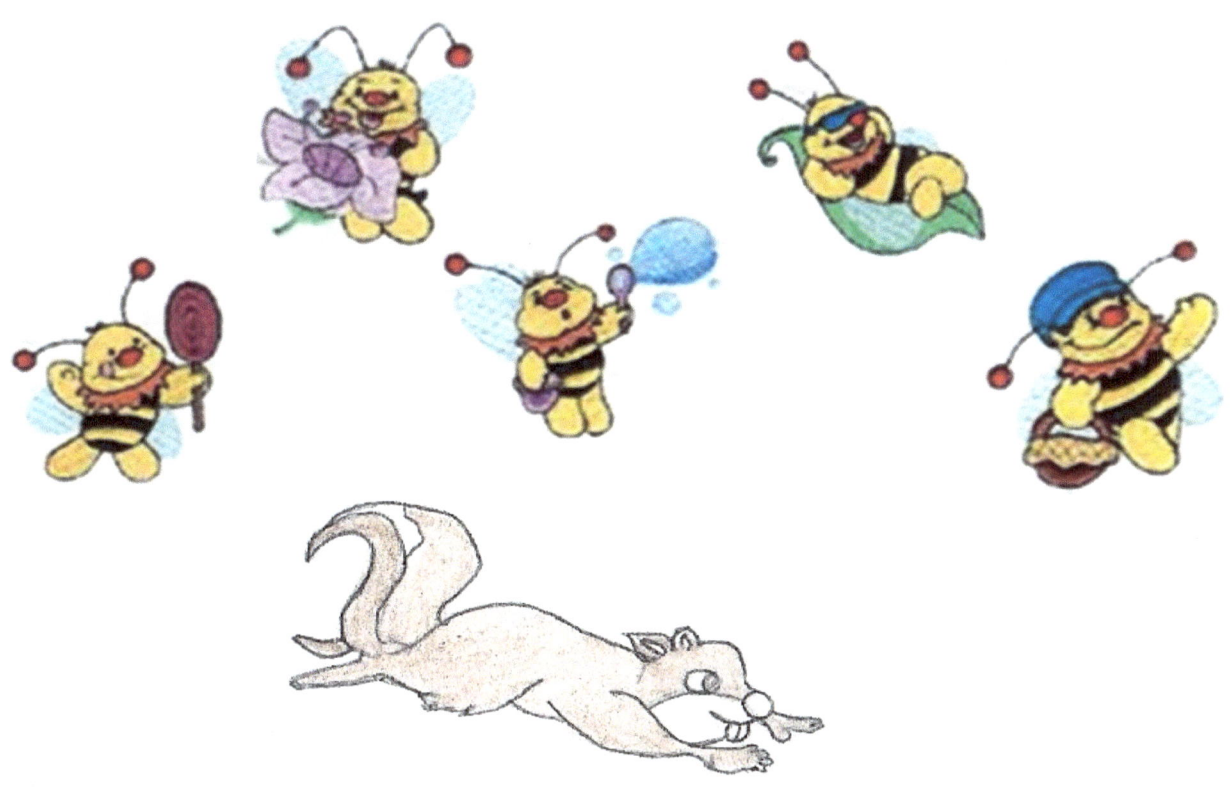

As Queeny came out of the beehive she asked Jerry what had happened. "There's some people stranded in a car on the highway, we have to hurry back to help them as quickly as possible."

The rest of the Humblebees also heard what Jerry said and agreed that they would try to help out. "Show us where they're at Jerry so that we can help them, said Starry. And with that, he started to run through the snow to show the Humblebees where the Hunters were at.

Ch.5 On Christmas Day

The Humblebees and Jerry to the Rescue!

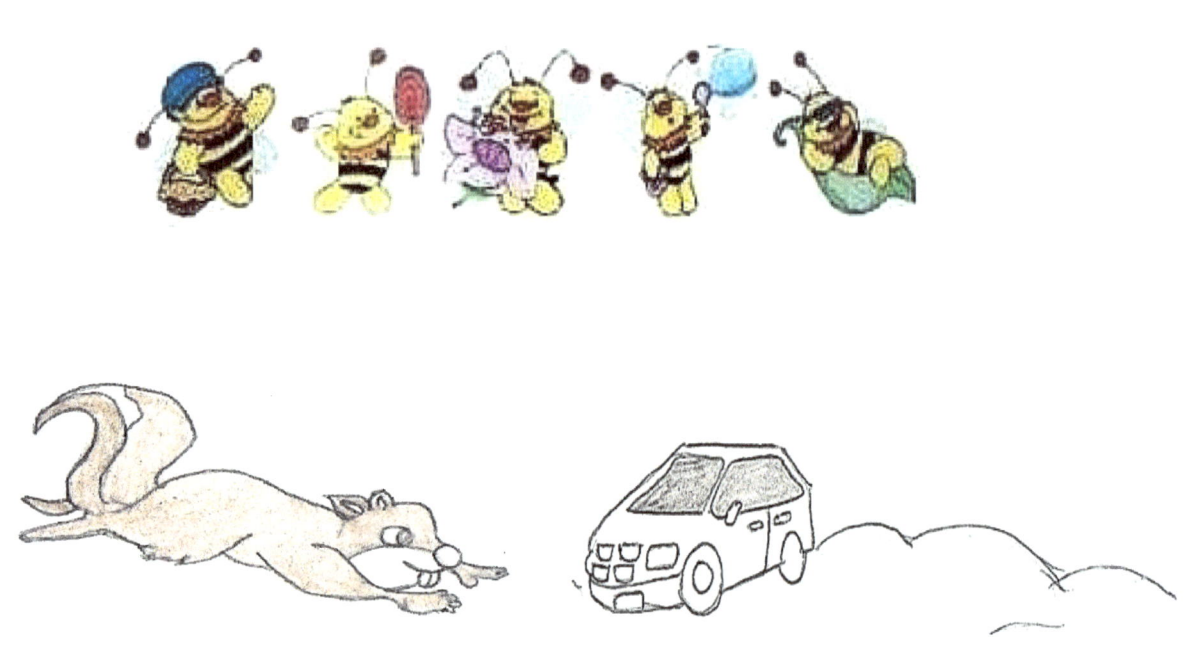

Mr. Hunter got out of the car to look at the tire. It was very hard to see because it was dark. Before he could get back into the car, he heard the scattering of a small animal coming his way. Jerry the squirrel had arrived with the Humblebees to try and help them. Ronnie and Jessica watched from the window as they surrounded the back of the car. Hi my name is Starry, we're the Humblebees and this is Jerry the squirrel.

We heard you folks were stranded and we're here to help you out"! Mr. Hunter could not believe his eyes or his ears and said "How can you help us, you are a bee and he's a squirrel that talks!" "We are magical, friendly bees," said Starry; "whenever we hear of someone in danger, we come to their rescue!"

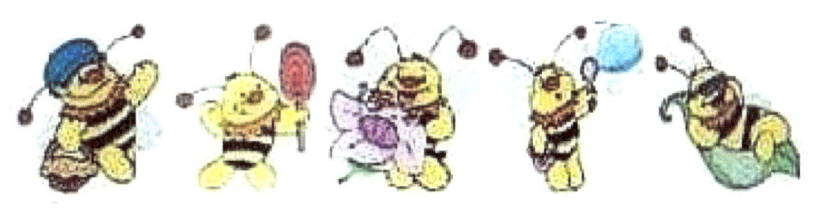

The Humblebees helping out!

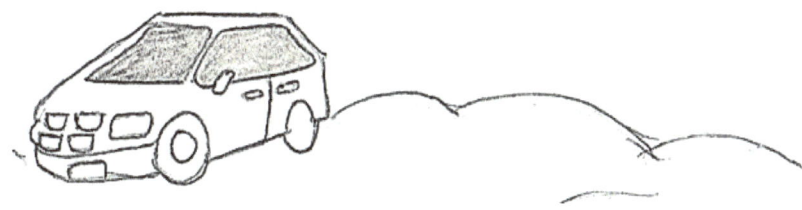

" I have a flat tire and I need a light to change it," said Mr. Hunter. "If you need some light, we can help you with that; here let us show you," said Queeny. As the Humblebees formed in a circle, a ray of light started to show all around the car. Jessica, Ronnie and Mrs. Hunter were very happy that the Humblebees had come as Ronnie yell out "Yea Humblebees, you're the greatest!"

The light was bright enough to help Mr. Hunter fix his tire to help them on their way. After the tire got fixed, Mr. Hunter, Mrs. Hunter, Jessica and Ronnie wanted to show the Humblebees how thankful they were for helping them on this cold winter night. "Thank you Humblebees so much for giving us a hand; if you want, you guys are welcomed to spend Christmas with us. We're on our way to visit Mrs. Hunter's mother, I'm sure that she won't mind"

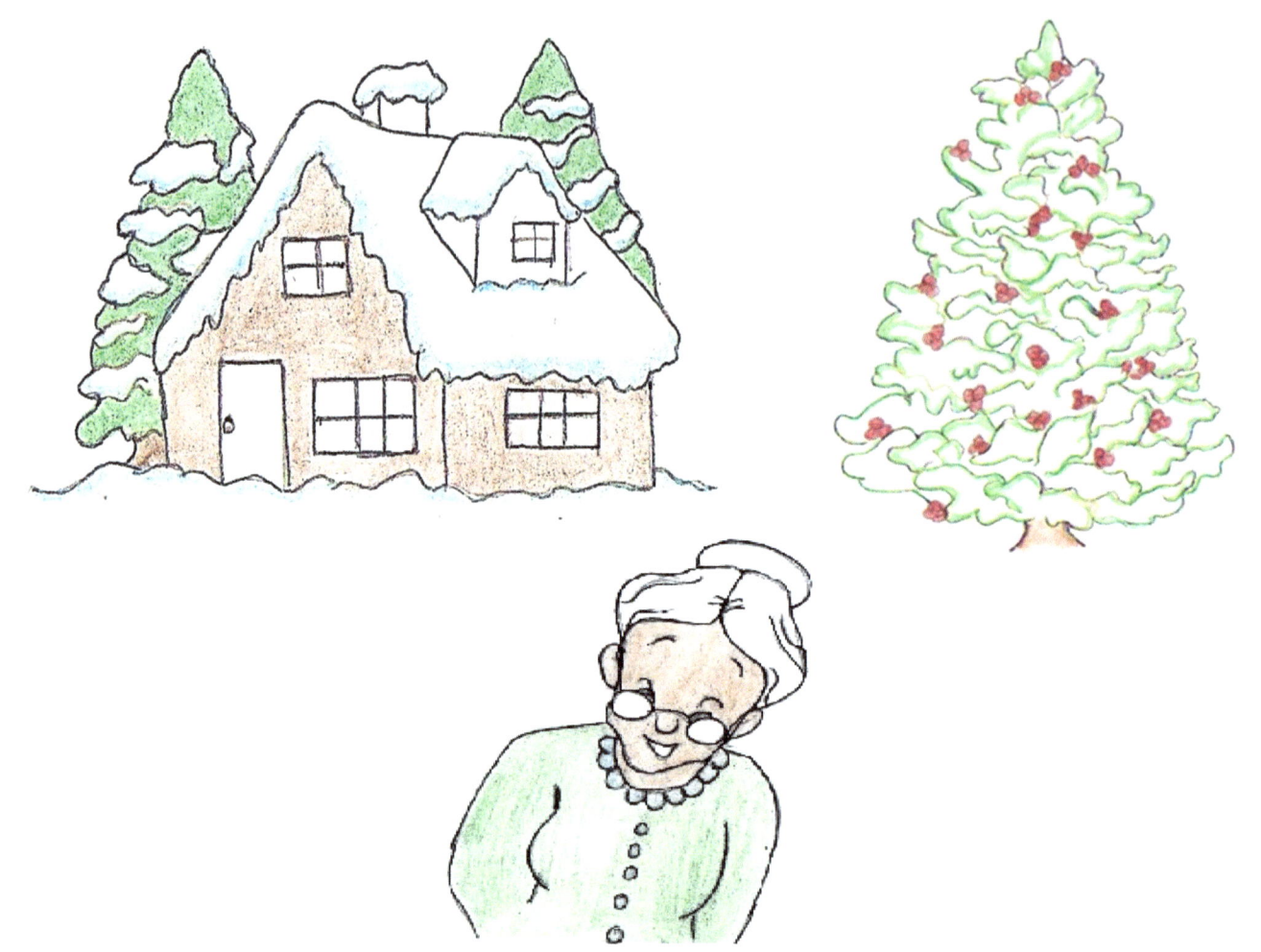

Grandmother

Jerry the squirrel had to go because the rest of his family was waiting for him, but the Humblebees said that they would escort the Hunter's to their grandmother's house. Everyone said goodbye to Jerry as Mr. and Mrs. Hunter, Jessica and Ronnie climbed back into their car to finish the trip. The Humblebees were flying over the car to make sure that they arrived at grandma's house safely.

Once they got there, grandma stood waiting at the door for them to come in. "My my, it took you a while to get here; was traffic heavy"? said grandma. No, we had a flat tire and we had to wait for someone to come and help us" said Mrs. Hunter.

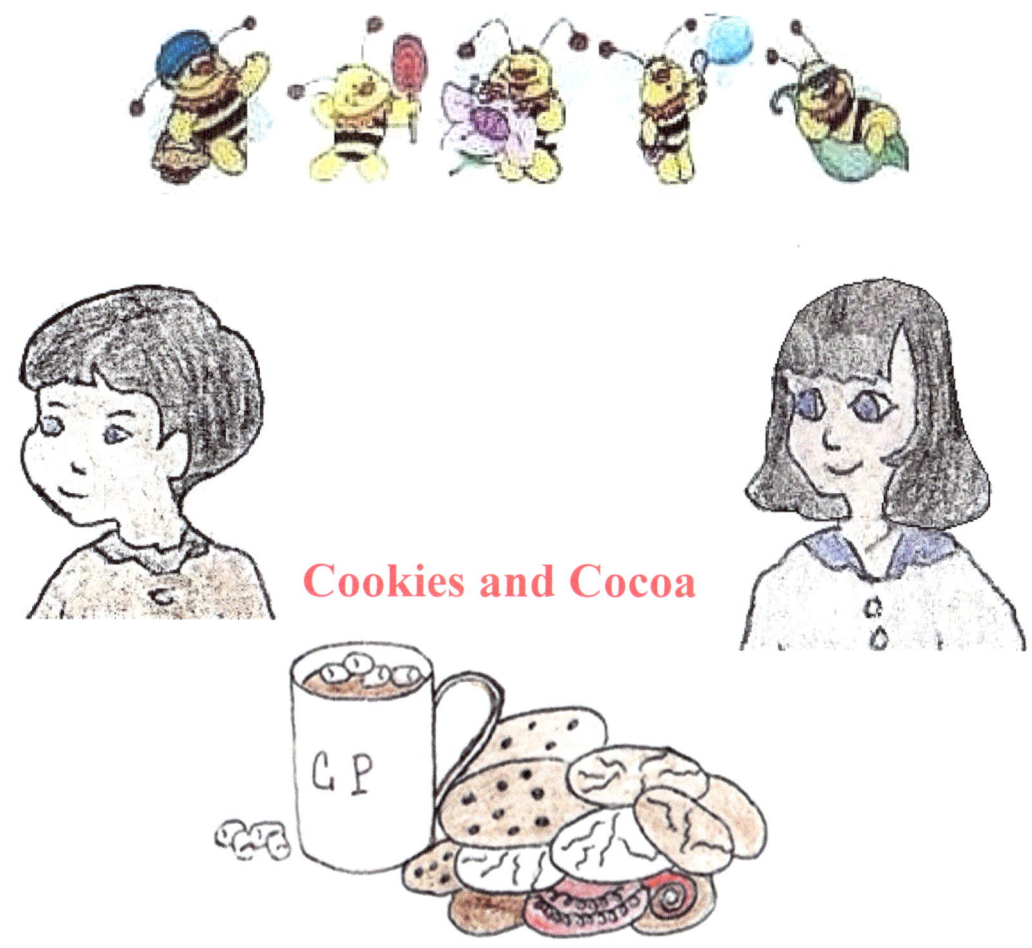

Cookies and Cocoa

"Well I'm glad that someone was able to help, my goodness children come on in and put your coats away, I have hot cocoa and cookies waiting for you." Then grandma also noticed that there were now bees in the house and started to get her broom. "No no mother, said Mrs. Hunter, they're our friends; they helped give us light to fix the flat tire."

"Yes, they certainly did" said Mr. Hunter. "Hello" said Starry as the rest of the Humblebees greeted her too. "Bees that talk, my my I can't believe it and they helped too"? said grandma "Yes, and we invited them to come spend Christmas with us to say thank you, said Jessica.

16

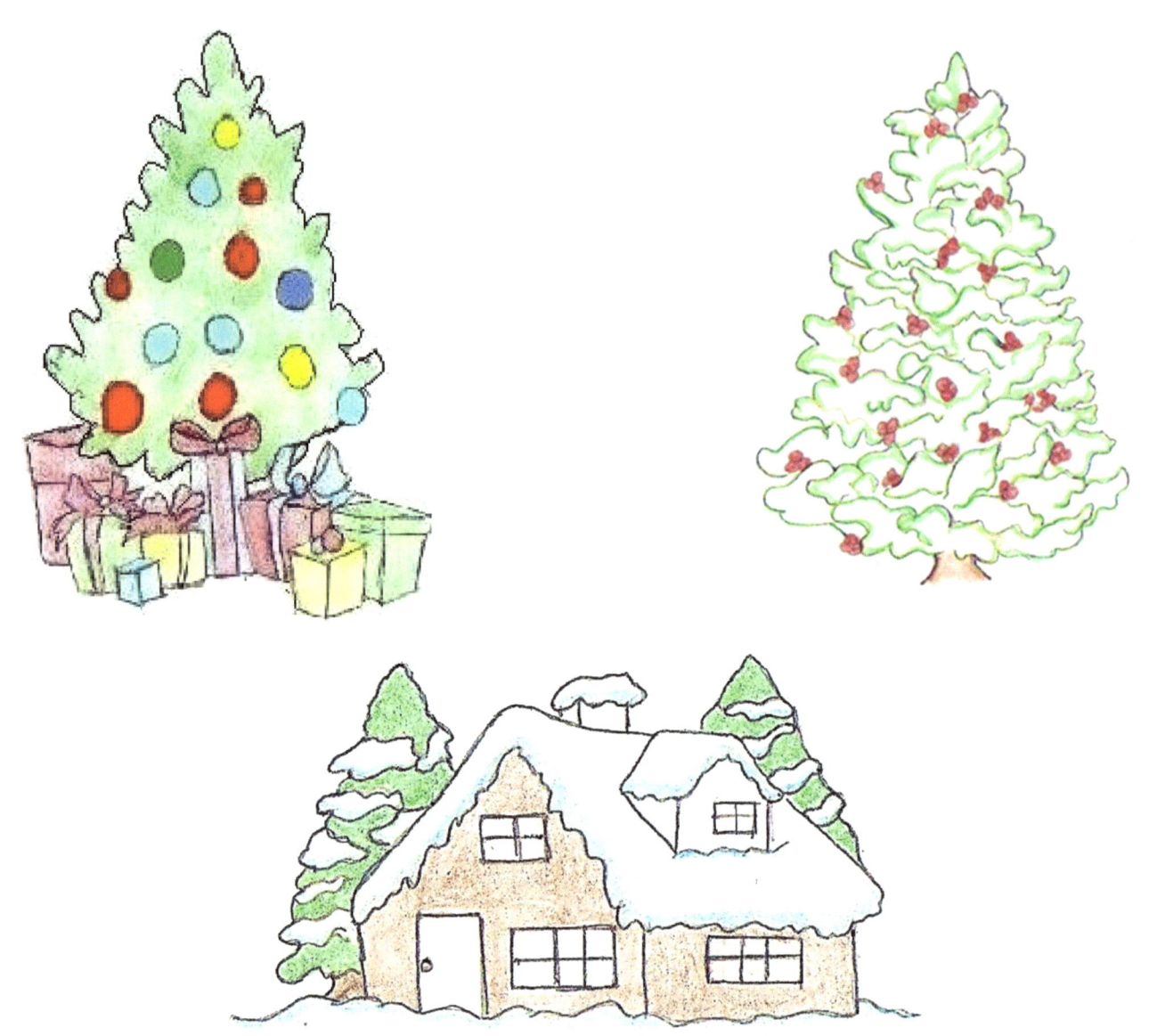

Because it took so long to get to grandma's house, it was now pass twelve o'clock on Christmas day. As Jessica and Ronnie changed into their pajamas, they joined everybody in the front room. "Humblebees, thank you so much for helping my family to drive here safely" said grandma. "Yes thank you again said the Hunter's. "Alright everyone gather around and let's sing our Christmas song that we sing every year said Mrs. Hunter. The Humblebees flew in closer to join the family. And they sanged "To everyone everywhere far and wide, *"We wish you a Merry Christmas, we wish you a merry Christmas, we wish you a merry Christmas ………and a Happy New Year"!!!*

The End

17

Humblebees illustrations by Design Stitch www.DesignStitch.com and Sensational Stitches www.SensationalStitches.ca Additional Illustrations by Cheryl Powe w/Assistant Book Cover Creator Lamika Powe

Away In A Manger

♫......Away in a manger, no crib for a bed; the little Lord Jesus asleep in the hay...the stars in the sky looked down where he lay, the little Lord Jesus asleep in the hay! The cattle are lowing, the baby awakes, But little Lord Jesus no crying he makes. I love Thee, Lord Jesus, look down from the sky And stay by my cradle til morning is nigh. Be near me, Lord Jesus, I ask Thee to stay Close by me forever, and love me, I pray. Bless all the dear children in thy tender care, And take us to heaven, to live with Thee there.♫

O' Little Town of Bethlehem

♫ O little town of Bethlehem, How still we see thee lie! Above thy

deep and dreamless sleep, The silent stars go by. Yet in thy dark

streets shineth The everlasting Light. The hopes and fears of all the

years Are met in thee tonight.♫

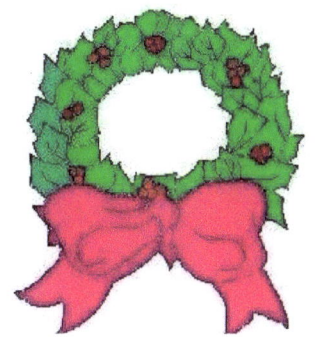 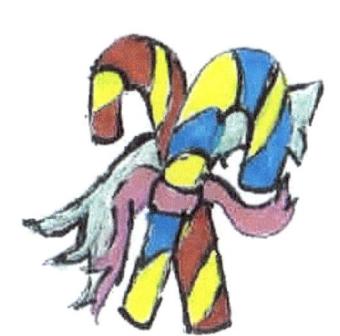 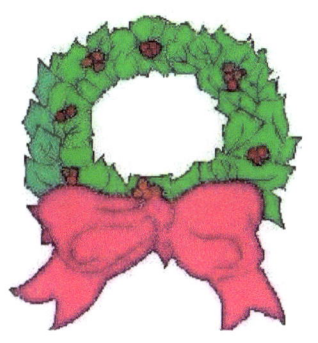

Merry Christmas!

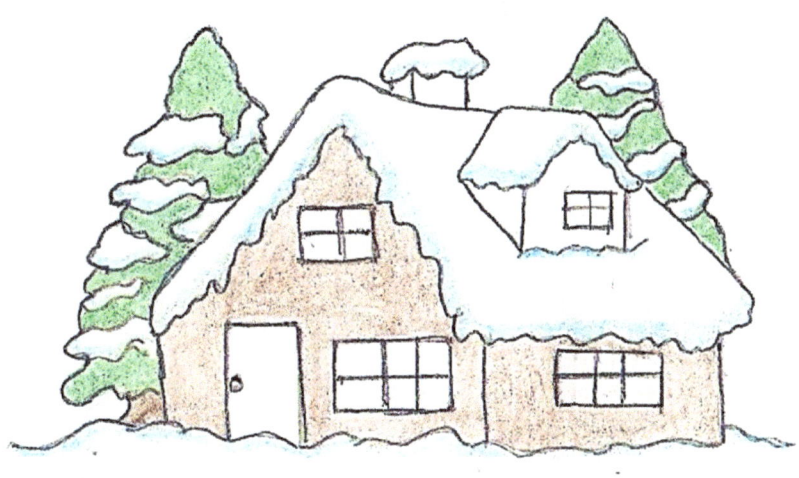